A MAN CALLED JESUS

LEARNING WITH JESUS SERIES
BOOK ONE(1)

WRITTEN BY
OLUWAFIAGBARAKUNMI .O

ISBN: 9798831861532

DEDICATION

I DEDICATE THIS BOOK TO GOD THE FATHER, JESUS CHRIST THE SON AND THE HOLY SPIRIT. ALSO TO MY LITTLE PRINCESS, CELESTINA WHOM AS WELL AS OTHER LITTLE ONES OUT THERE, I WANT TO GIVE AS MUCH AS I POSSIBLY CAN, A GOOD UNDERSTANDING OF GOD AND OUR LORD, JESUS CHRIST'S SACRIFICE AND HIS LOVE FOR US.

To every little one out there, I want you to know that Jesus is the best friend you can ever have and life with him is the best because you will have him to walk with you through life. Yours truly, Oluwafiagbarakunmi☺

Hello little one, my name
is Jesus. I am the son of
God and he has sent me
to save the world teach
you his words and how to
be good children. What is
your name?

Jesus came to earth thousands of years ago, he did many wonders and the biggest of them all was dying on the cross, he resurrected and gave us salvation.

These wonders gave Jesus a lot of sweet names which he will be sharing with us.

Together, we will be
using the alphabet A-Z to
help you learn more
about Jesus.

A - Alpha

I am the Alpha and Omega. Alpha means the first or the beginning.

Revelations 22:13

 **- Bread of life**

I am the bread of life.
Come to me and you shall
never go hungry.

John 6:35

C

- Chief corner stone.

He is our guide and foundation.

Ephesians 2: 20

D
- Our deliverer

Jesus is the truth and the truth shall set you free.

John 8:32

E

- Eternal life.

Anyone who receives
me with open arms,
receives eternal life.

1 John 1: 2

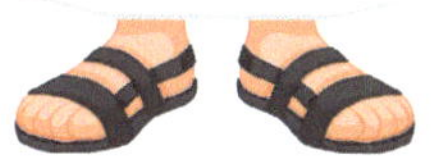

F

- Fountain of life.

Anyone who believes
in me will be saved.
John 7: 38

G

– the Gate

Anyone who comes through me will have access to the Father.

John 10: 9

H - Healer

I heal all disease and pain.

Matthew 9: 35

I

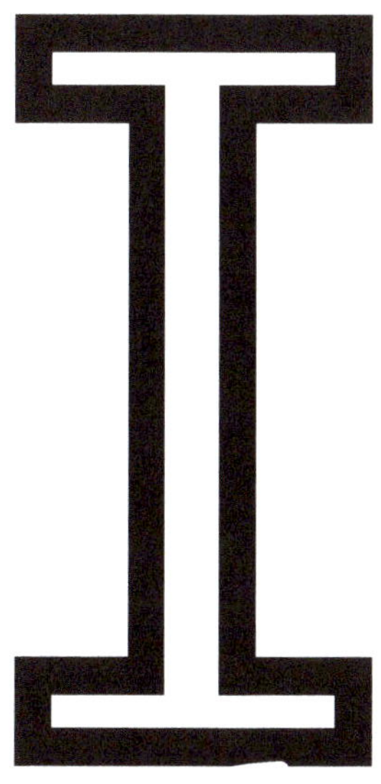

- Immanuel

His birth still remains
a wonder.
"Immanuel means
God with us."

Isaiah 7:14

J

- our Justifier.

I am always here to
defend you.

Romans 3: 26

K

- King of kings.

He rules above all
kings.

Revelation 19: 16

L

- Lamb of God.

His sacrifice on the cross freed us from sin.

John 1: 29

M  - Messiah

I am Christ, teacher
of all things.

John 4:25- 26

N- a Name above all names.

God, my father gave me a name greater than any other name that every knee shall bow at the mention of it.
Phillipians 2: 9

O

- Offspring of David.

I am from a lineage
of great men.
Rev 22: 16

P

- Prince of peace.

A government rests
upon his shoulder.

Isaiah 9: 6

Q - Quieter of storms.

I am able to calm every worry in your heart.

Matthew 8: 27

R - the Redeemer

He is always there
to help us when
we are in trouble.
Psalms 18: 2

Will you call him
when in trouble?

Yes / No

S

– our Saviour

He was born and
died so we can be
saved.

Luke 2: 11

T

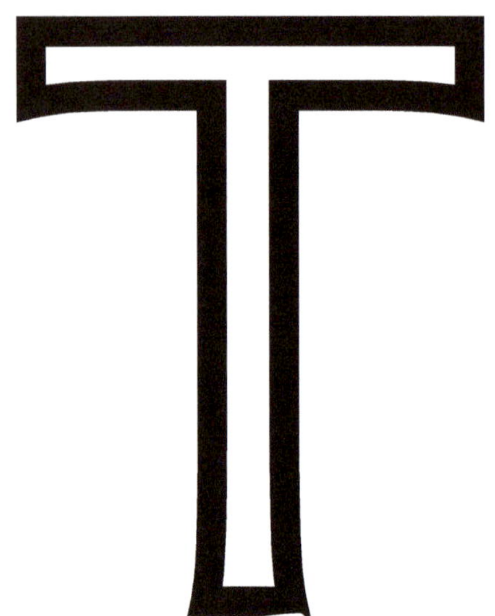

- the Truth.

I am the truth, know
the truth and you
shall be set free.

John 8: 32

U - Undefeatable warrior.

I am the Lord,strong and mighty in battle. I am here to fight all your battles even those unseen.

Psalms 24: 8

V

- the true Vine.

I am the true vine
and my father is the
gardener.

John 15: 1

W

- the Way.

To access the Father,
you need to go
through me.
Would you like to be
my friend?

John 14: 6

Yes / No

X

\- Xray to our heart/soul.

I am the word of God and a seer of all your thoughts, good or bad.

Hebrews 4: 12

I want you to always think of good things.

Y

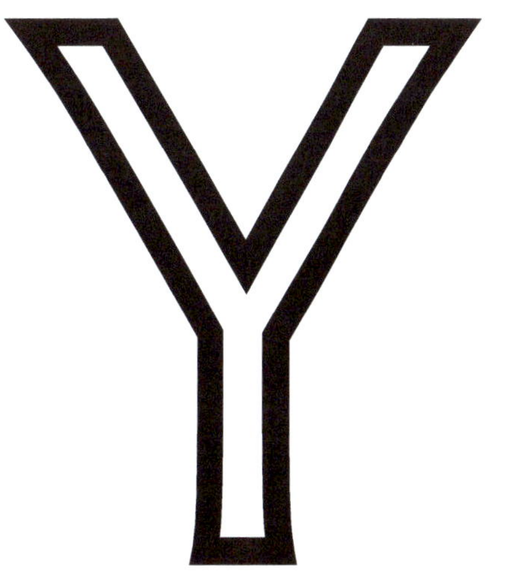

- Yeshua

This is his Hebrew name in English letters, meaning "to resue/to save". (This name is used in the hebrew bible and original king James version bible)

Z

Z - Zion's glory.

Before Jesus was
sent to the world,
the old prophets had
forseen his coming.

Psalms 53:6

I believe you know me well now. Would you love to be my friend? If yes, let's continue this adventure in book two(2) of the learning with Jesus series new words with the alphabet A-Z and their meanings.

❤ from
your best friend, Jesus.

www.ingramcontent.com/pod-product-compliance
Lightning Source LLC
Chambersburg PA
CBHW040931110726
48006CB00001B/151